Guns Are Not Our God - The NRA Is Not Our Church!

In support of

#MarchForOurLives

&

#NationalSchoolWalkout

By

Ravi Chandra, M.D.

Guns Are Not Our God - The NRA Is Not Our Church!
In Support of #MarchForOurLives and
#NationalSchoolWalkout

Pacific Heart Books
San Francisco, CA
www.ravichandramd.com

Copyright © 2018 by Ravi Chandra. All rights reserved.
Ravi Chandra and Pacific Heart Books support copyright.
No part of this book may be reproduced in any form or by
any means, electronic or mechanical, including photocopying,
recording, or by any information storage and retrieval system,
without permission in writing from the publisher, except for
brief quotations for review or academic purposes.

ISBN: 978-0-9909339-4-6 (Paperback edition)
ISBN: 978-0-9909339-5-3 (eBook edition)

Library of Congress Control Number: 2018936359

Jacket design by Việt Lê
Interior design by Integrative Ink

A portion of proceeds from sale of this book will go to
organizations supporting mental health and gun control.

*In memory of lives lost
every day*

and dedicated to the young student leaders
of Marjory Stoneman Douglas
and schools across this wonderful country

Table of Contents

**Guns Are Not Our God -
The NRA Is Not Our Church!** 1

Guns are a major threat to the lives of all
Americans, regardless of race, gender or class 4

The public health rationale for
gun control is clear 11

Mental illness and gun deaths 15

Gun identity and the American identity crisis:
Gaslighting the nation, and examples of
change from abroad 23

Guns, race and identity in American culture 32

Identity, guns and transcendence 41

Conclusions 62

Gun Attitude Scale 72

Endnotes 75

Acknowledgments 85

About the Author 87

Guns Are Not Our God - The NRA Is Not Our Church!

> A well regulated Militia, being necessary to the security of a free State, the right of the people to keep and bear Arms, shall not be infringed.
>
> — The Second Amendment to the Constitution of the United States, 1789

THE INDIVIDUAL RIGHT TO bear arms was advanced by a narrow 5 to 4 U.S. Supreme Court decision in *District of Columbia v. Heller* in 2008, but the primal, seemingly hardwired and instinctive demand and rage for guns are part of our national psychological constitution as well. Guns seem integral to the identities of many Americans. Any proposal to restrict or regulate ownership is met with such ferocious resistance by some gun owners that one might think one had proposed amputating a part of their anatomy. Castration, perhaps, symbolically, given how guns are linked with American masculinity. Or worse. In fact, gun control legislation threatens death, destruction and annihilation to a certain kind of American identity.

The NRA (National Rifle Association) seems to now view even common sense gun regulation as a death threat to its idea of America. Or, more cynically, a death threat to the bottom lines of gun manufacturers, now fused with the survival of the American Individualist himself. If your basic existential fear and philosophy is "kill or be killed," one man in vital struggle with menacing others, then it becomes clear why others would have to take this gun "from my cold dead hands," as Charlton Heston said in the run-up to the 2000 presidential election. (In fact, NRA opposition cost Al Gore his home state of Tennessee, Florida and possibly the election, thus affirming our national gun identity.)

Surely, Justice Antonin Scalia's finding of an individual right to bear arms for the purpose of self-defense was as much based on his biases about the American self in apposition to communal and governmental concerns as it was on his reading of the U.S. Constitution and history. His defense of the Second Amendment was not just about self-defense, but about defense of the American self.

Changing the country's ideas about guns will involve transforming and transcending American identity, and embracing a different idea of American selfhood, one based on compassion, interdependence and the public good. It is a hopeful selfhood, not a selfhood warily scanning the horizon for apocalypse and reflexively mistrusting any and all external authority, as well as fearing and hating people of color. At the very least, we will have to break the NRA's stranglehold on American politics.

We've had the logic of statistics, the emotions of seeing innocents die, the public health rationales of experts – but nothing has yet swayed the outcome of this debate. This can only be because we have been hijacked by a cabal of irrational gun identitarians who put their absolute right to own guns ahead of any sensible limits, ahead of the lives of others. They have put substantial money and often vicious energy to work, their self-centered right against the public well-being. Nothing short of national transformation will be good enough to overcome them. Gun regulations are a death threat to their way of life.

But we must all face our death threats, and decide how we wish to live, together.

Guns are a major threat to the lives of all Americans, regardless of race, gender or class

GLOBALLY, GUNS ARE USED in 40% of all homicides.[1] In the U.S., the figure is 64%.[2] The United States is the most heavily armed developed nation in the world. 30% of us own guns. 42% of households report gun ownership. At least 2/3rds of Americans report having lived in a household with a gun at some point in their lives.[3] Seven in ten report having fired a gun at least once. Half of White men report gun ownership, twice the rate of non-White men and White women, and three times the rate of non-White women. The U.S. has only 4% of the world's population, but 31% of its guns. U.S. guns are also smuggled into other countries, and are therefore linked to international violence. In this country, we collectively hold over 350 million guns, more than one for every man, woman, infant and child. Guns, therefore, have a special, exalted (and some would say morbid and strange) significance for individuals in our society. But if gun ownership is the norm, then it is a malignant normality.

Firearms cause about 32,000 fatalities annually in the United States. Of these about 19,000 are suicides and 13,000 are homicides, accidental deaths or war casualties. Another 74,000 people are injured by gunshots. 44% of us know a gunshot victim, myself included. The first newly dead body I saw was a gunshot victim in the Stanford ER, a White woman I'll never forget, whose naked body was contorted and frozen, arms and legs stretched upwards as if she was falling into a forever-hole. My friend and medical school classmate, Rich Walker, committed suicide with a rifle while in surgical residency training. And my fellow poet and friend, Itzolin Garcia, committed suicide with a handgun while I was a psychiatry resident. I still mourn them, still wish I'd been able to help.

Homicide risk by firearm is highest for young Black men, suicide risk by gun highest for older White men. The 16-state National Violent Death Reporting System indicates that 51.8% of suicides in 2009 were firearm-related, almost twice as high as the next highest Western industrialized country, Sweden, even though Sweden has a higher overall suicide rate. Guns are more deadly here in the U.S. Suicide is the third highest cause of death in 15-24 year olds in the U.S. The U.S. has the highest reported rate of suicides by firearm, at 6.3 per 100,000 population. Our annual rate of firearm homicide is the highest of any high-income nation, at over 3 per 100,000. 66.5% of homicides were firearm-related. The U.S. gun homicide rate is 25.2 times higher than other developed nations, and 49 times higher for 15-24 year olds.

Suicide is impulsive, and not limited to those with mental illness. The odds risk for suicide for those with guns in the home is 3.24 times higher than those without guns in the home. The risk is greatest (13x) for those without mental illness.[4] Suicide risk goes up if firearms are kept unlocked or loaded. Adolescent suicide victims are more likely to used an unlocked firearm kept in the home. Among adolescents with a suicide plan, those with firearms in the house were seven times more likely to have a plan involving firearms.[5] 93% of suicide attempts involving guns result in death.

The odds risk for homicide is 2.0 for those with guns in the home.[6] Risk of homicide goes up 20-fold if there's a history of domestic violence.[7] Like suicide, impulsivity may play a role in homicide as well, particularly the killing of women by their abusive partners in their homes.[8] Ominously, in at least 10% of households with children surveyed, the female partner did not know the male partner had a gun, putting both her and the children at risk.[9] It's possible that even more women without children are unaware of their male partner's gun ownership. The risk of gun homicide increases with a history of domestic violence. It's not only important to screen for such violence, but also remove guns from the homes of batterers.

Many people claim that they keep guns in the home for protection, but research suggests this is counterproductive. Nationally, less than 1% of gun homicides were committed in self-defense, and a similarly small percentage were cited as having been used to resist potential attackers.[10] 76.4% of gun suicides occurred in victims' homes. 74% of female gun homicide victims were killed at home, and 45.5% of male victims were killed at home. Kellerman *et al* state, after studying several hundred domestic homicides in three countries:

> "despite the widely held belief that guns are effective for protection, our results suggest that they actually pose a substantial threat to members of the household. People who keep guns in their homes appear to be at greater risk of homicide in the home than people who do not. Most of this risk is due to a substantially greater risk of homicide at the hands of a family member or intimate acquaintance. We did not find evidence of a protective effect of keeping a gun in the home, even in the small subgroup

of cases that involved forced entry...**People should be strongly discouraged from keeping guns in their homes.**" (RC - emphasis mine.)

Our inability to control gun violence, our willingness to accept apathy on all public health measures involving gun control, is also an example of racism at work. Homicide is the leading cause of death amongst Blacks aged 10-24. The homicide rate for black victims (16.3 per 100,000) was 6 times higher than the homicide rate for whites (2.6 per 100,000). The overall national homicide rate is 4.4 per 100,000.[11] Exposure to gun violence is correlated with worsened physical and emotional health, even years later. Violence also perpetuates, and is linked in a vicious cycle with, poverty. From Byrdsong *et al*:

> "Over the past 20 years, Community Empowerment Association (CEA) has observed how gun violence erodes communities in many ways: by reducing public safety, tumbling economic and business activities, devaluing properties, and ruining the quality of life of people of all ages. It has also seriously disrupted youth education, lowered neighborhood attachment,

and strained family relationships. In addition, most survivors of violence bear permanent physical and emotional scars."

The authors prescribe detailed community public health interventions to reduce gun violence and minimize its harmful effects, with prevention, rehabilitation and community development their cornerstones. They pointedly suggest that simply attacking the problem with aggressive law enforcement will not work, based on their community work and analysis. Clearly, one prong of prevention is reducing access to firearms on a national basis.

Most firearms used in youth homicide are obtained illegally. Of adolescents presenting for assault in one sample, there was a gun carriage rate of 41.5%.[12] 1/4th of those were "automatic/semiautomatic weapons that are large clip, high rate-of-fire weapons, or may be modified to these highly lethal weapon types." Improving policies around production and access to these and other guns is key. Our willingness to turn a blind eye to violence affecting people of color is a direct mechanism of racist action by the gun lobby. But White males not on public assistance seeking care for assault are more likely to possess guns than their Black male counterparts on public aid. This affects all of us.

The public health rationale for gun control is clear

STATES WITH HIGHER PERCENTAGES of households owning guns tend to have higher gun fatality rates.[13] Gun regulations that aim at restricting and reducing gun ownership reduce firearm suicide rates. Anestis, Anestis and Butterworth studied[14] suicide rate changes in 2013 and 2014 in all 50 states and the District of Columbia, comparing the rates in states with and without specific laws (mandatory waiting periods, universal background checks, open carry restrictions and gun lock requirements). They found significant difference in suicide rate changes in states with mandatory waiting periods and universal background checks relative to states without these laws. No changes were observed in states with open carry restrictions and gun lock requirements. They conclude that laws aimed at reducing gun ownership were the most effective at preventing firearm suicides. Of note, people denied guns do not typically then find other means of harming themselves. Suicide rates go down when gun ownership and storage is more regulated. Kposowa *et al* similarly found[15] that higher gun ownership increased suicide risk, but loaded and unlocked guns in the home were an even more powerful risk factor. Guns are a suicide magnet, and gun regulations and safe storage make a big difference.

Fleegler *et al* came to similar conclusions about firearm laws and overall fatalities, both suicides and homicides.[16] They looked at all 50 states over four years, dividing the states into quartiles based on their gun regulations. The quartile with the most regulations had the lowest gun homicide and suicide rates, and the states with the least regulations had the highest gun homicide and suicide rates. However, the authors could not conclude the link was a direct cause and effect. There could be other factors working in these states, for example different levels of gun ownership or different attitutes towards guns, which both make it more difficult to pass gun laws and more likely that guns will be used. Still, working towards stronger gun laws would be helpful, and could clarify these other factors.

Kalesan *et al* looked[17] at 25 firearm laws across the United States, and analyzed their correlation with firearm mortalities. They found that the three laws most significantly associated with reduced mortality were universal background checks for guns, background checks for ammunition and requiring firearm identification by microstamping or ballistic fingerprinting. While their analysis of the magnitude of the effect is complicated and to some, controversial, they estimate that these laws could reduce firearm fatalities by 90%. They also found that so-called "stand your ground" laws were associated with *increased* mortality rates.

Gun ownership increases risk of fatalities, and families with risk factors for suicide and homicide are modestly *more* likely to own guns.[18] Parents with depression, who binge drink or use illicit drugs are more likely to have or acquire guns. This puts them and their children at risk. The mental health system might play a role in treating the risk factors, or screening for firearms in these homes, but this makes the regulations described by the above authors, like waiting periods and background checks, all the more salient.

In addition to gun control legislation and reducing the number of firearms on the street, there may be other ways to cut gun violence. Public health experts have looked at how gun violence spreads as social contagion, through a network of individuals embedded in the same relationships, activities and environment, thus sharing risk factors. A preventive approach might be akin to contact tracing used in disease outbreaks.[19] We could also encourage the media not to cover shootings in sensationalistic ways that inspire copycats.[20]

The American Psychiatric Association, American Academy of Family Physicians, American Academy of Pediatrics, and American Congress of Obstetricians and Gynecologists, representing a total of 450,000 physicians, have all called for governmental action on the epidemic of gun violence.[21] Rationally, gun control makes sense. But instead, those who support gun ownership usually throw the first stones at those with mental health problems.

Mental illness and gun deaths

IT'S TRUE THAT MENTALLY ill populations are at higher risk for committing violence, particularly those with personality, substance abuse and psychotic disorders. Research indicates that those with schizophrenia commit homicide thirteen times more often than the general population,[22] with the risk increased for those with untreated illness, substance abuse, situational and demographic factors, and past violence.[23] For all mental illness combined, those with mental illness and substance abuse commit violence at a rate four times higher than those without mental illness (7-8% vs 2%). Lifetime rates of violence are estimated at 15% for those without mental illness, 33% for those with mental illness, and 55% for those with both mental illness and substance abuse.[24] But studies "confirm that most violent individuals do not have mental illness, and that the vast majority of individuals with mental illness (even those with the aforementioned illnesses) are not violent. **They are more likely to be victims not perpetrators of violence.**" A clinician predicting violence in a person with depression and substance abuse disorder, for example, would statistically be wrong 90% of the time.[25] (Other demographic factors such as age, race, gender and socioeconomic status would improve accuracy, just as it would for the general population, but not the presence of illness alone.) 25% of those with mental illness are likely to be victims of violence, compared to 3% of the general population.[26] We would do better to screen the mentally ill for their experiences and risks of being victims of violence, rather than solely focusing on screening them for committing violence. Some propose creating a national database of all mentally ill for gun control purposes. Besides concerns over invasion of privacy, civil rights and stigmatization of perhaps a third of the population (depending on how broad one's definition is), any such list would be more accurately called a list of potential victims of violence at high-risk, worthy of additional protection.

Violence is not primarily a problem of mental illness. The annual attributable risk of mental illness to violence in the United States is only 2-4%. Age and gender are much better predictors. 75% of violent crimes are committed by males under the age of 18. More than 95% of gun homicides are perpetrated by those without a mental illness.[27] Out of 133 mass murders between January, 2009 and July, 2015, only one of the murderers had been prohibited from owning guns due to mental illness, and in only 11% of shootings had concerns about the shooter's mental health been brought to an authority.[28] In fact, as Metzl and Macleish note,

> "Psychiatric diagnosis is in and of itself not predictive of violence, and even the overwhelming majority of psychiatric patients who fit the profile of recent U.S. mass shooters –

gun-owning, angry, paranoid White men – do not commit crimes."[29]

We'll get back to that particular identity – gun-owning, angry, paranoid White men – later.

Still, as Choe *et al* write, "(d)espite the small attributable risk of severe mental disorders on violent perpetration, negative stereotypes of persons with severe mental illness dominate the public's view and behavioral scientists' focus." Every time someone talks about mental health as a primary factor in violence, they are perpetuating dangerous and inaccurate stereotypes that could potentially lead to victimization of those with mental health issues. President Trump, Stigmatizer-in-Chief, exemplified this in his proposal to hospitalize more patients. "We've got to get them out of our communities," he said, casting a shadow over all those who suffer mental illness.[30] "Nab the sickos," he urged; ironic, considering many professionals consider the president himself dangerous and sick.[31] Certainly, chronic care facilities would be good treatment for some of the more gravely disabled – but it is not a credible mechanism of significantly reducing our chart-busting epidemic of gun violence. To reiterate: a small minority of mentally ill persons are dangerous. Moreover, it's extremely difficult to accurately predict violence in a mentally ill person. The vast majority of violence is committed by those without mental illness, and the main predictor for future violence is past violence. Screening for this by implementing universal background checks, in addition to preventing access for those whom mental health professionals deem to be at risk, would be better than stigmatizing all those with mental health issues.

The National Instant Criminal Background Check System (NICS) was implemented in 1998 and improved in 2008, after the Virginia Tech massacre. In 2013, almost a third of those denied guns were denied due to mental illness history, definitely a positive development. Still, "more than 99% of gun-disqualifying mental health records archived in the NICS have not resulted in any denials of attempted firearms purchases by prohibited individuals."[32] These are presumably ill people who choose not to purchase weapons. Also, many of the mentally ill at risk of violence do not have records in the system, because they have not yet presented for care or they were admitted to a private hospital, for example. Also, many people already have access to guns in the home, so they do not need to purchase a weapon. For example, Adam Lanza, the Sandy Hook shooter. Some states have implemented policies of gun removal under the recommendation of a mental health professional or others. Effects of these laws have not been well studied, to my knowledge. However, one could see that they might deter some people from seeking care.

Expert medical opinion is clear on the path to reducing gun violence:[33] restricting access to guns (with waiting periods, minimum age, safety training and other permit requirements, safe storage requirements, etc). Focusing on mental illness alone as a predisposing factor will not reduce homicide, but will only serve to stigmatize and distract.[34] Even if all people with mental illness were denied guns, immediately and irrevocably, the homicide rate would likely not be much affected, though suicides would decrease. The violence rate would drop by less than 4%. Backing this up, a survey of 27 developed countries found "gun ownership was a significant predictor of firearm-related deaths, whereas mental illness was of borderline significance."[35] Reduce gun ownership in the population, and you reduce fatalities. Simple. But do we have heart enough to save lives rather than saving our guns? Or will we proceed to "harden our schools," as President Trump and the NRA propose, and in so doing, harden our hearts? It is a question of morals, but also of identity and transcendence. Who are we? Who are we to each other? The gun debate highlights our American identity crisis.

In summary, mental illness is a distraction and red herring in the gun debate. A focus on the mentally ill does not capture the real nature of the problem, and is, as Drs. Dudley *et al* from Australia write, "a calculated appeal to prejudice." Certainly, clinicians must become better at predicting risk for suicide and homicide. But we must think about gun violence practically and strategically, and also widen our inquiry into the nature of violence. Once again, from Metzl and Macleish:

> "Insanity becomes the only politically 'sane' (RC – quotes mine) place to discuss gun control. Meanwhile, a host of other narratives, such as displaced male anxiety about demographic change, the mass psychology of needing so many guns in the first place, or the symptoms created by being surrounded by them, remain unspoken."

We have an uphill battle though. 48% of Americans blame the mental health system for "a great deal" of the mass shootings, while only 40% blame easy access to guns.[36] "An inadequate mental health system is perceived as the top cause of mass shootings," only worsened by words of our President Trump and others. Certainly, we need to care better for people with mental health issues, and do better at identifying those who are both potential victims and perpetrators of violence. There are proposals from public health experts to do just this. But our problem with gun violence is not primarily a problem of mental illness. If there is mental illness involved, it is in our gun-crazed culture.

Gun identity and the American identity crisis: Gaslighting the nation, and examples of change from abroad

GUN IDENTITY HARDENED BY the NRA, not rationality, underlies opposition to gun control measures. Clinging to this identity creates a reality distortion bubble as gun identitarians and their allies attempt to gaslight the country and create their false narrative. At the very least, the gun identititarian tries to throw off the scent on the trail of responsible gun regulation, using all kinds of illogical, factually inaccurate and emotional arguments betraying only that they would say practically anything to defend their guns.[37] It's a sign of perhaps pathological self-centeredness, this unwillingness to consider that they are wrong. This happens even at the top. After the Parkland massacre on Valentine's Day, 2018, President Trump offered thoughts and prayers, counseled kindness, and called for mental health remedies. (He did later call for an NRA-supported ban on bump stocks which went nowhere when proposed the previous year after the Las Vegas massacre. He also called for some improvement in the background check system, which I predict will be weak improvements vetted by the NRA. The president voiced initial support for raising the age at which one could purchase assault rifles to 21, and alarmingly supported arming teachers and giving them bonuses for carrying weapons. Trump had also weakened some Obama era restrictions on gun purchases by fugitives and those deemed mentally ill, so his track record is not good.)[38]

Attorney General Jeff Sessions murkily admitted "it cannot be denied that something dangerous and unhealthy is happening in our country," but according to Sessions and other GOP partisans, that something is not guns. Legislators look both ways and whisper "something strange" is happening in this country, but we shouldn't "rush to judgment" about guns. What's strange is their performative capacity for denial and blame-shifting.

Matt Blevin, Republican governor of Kentucky, blamed video games, music and "evil," not guns, for mass shootings.[39] Rep. Ted Budd (R-NC), who owns a retail gun store, blamed[40] "radical Islamic terrorism" and the "mentally disturbed" for violence in America, not the unrestricted availability of guns. Tyler Tannahill, 2018 Republican candidate for Congress in Kansas, refused to cancel his AR-15 campaign giveaway, and other GOP candidates have offered similar giveaways in the past.[41] The gun identity is never in bad taste with these actors - implying that it is would be an admission of weakness. Bill O'Reilly said the media shouldn't pay attention to emotional teenagers. Rush Limbaugh and other ideologues claimed that protesting Parkland students were actually paid actors, or worse, that the massacre itself "was a 'false flag' orchestrated by anti-gun groups."[42] Limbaugh and others proclaimed that the answer was concealed carry and armed teachers in the schools, more "good guys with guns."[43] So goes the path to gun identity psychosis. To be fair, even when President Obama called for background checks in the wake of the Newtown massacre, a Democratic Senate did not back him. We are all affected by the insanity of guns.

Not so in other countries.

On March 13, 1996, a troubled and aggrieved 43 year old man walked into the Dunblane Primary School in Scotland with four legally-owned handguns and 743 cartridges of ammunition. He fatally shot 16 children and one teacher and wounded 16 others before killing himself. Public grief and outrage was immediate, inspiring a mass movement, the Snowdrop Campaign, to ban handguns. (The snowdrop blooms in March in Scotland.) Their petition garnered over 50,000 signatures in under six weeks. In less than two years, and under both Conservative and Labour party leadership, two extremely strict gun regulation measures were passed which effectively banned private ownership of all handguns throughout the U.K., except for Northern Ireland. Today, only muzzle-loading and historic handguns can be lawfully owned by individuals.[44]

In the 21 years since the Firearms Acts were passed, there has been only one mass shooting in the U.K., the 2010 Cumbria shootings (killing 11 and wounding 12). The firearm homicide rate in England and Wales is 1/30th the rate of the US.

The Australia story is perhaps more instructive, as Australia, like the U.S., was founded by settlers in a vast frontier, giving rise to individualism and similar affinity for guns. On April 28th-29th, 1996, a resentful, aggrieved 28 year old man with intellectual disabilities and limited empathic capacity, inspired by the Dunblane Massacre just six weeks prior, went on a rampage in Port Arthur, Tasmania, Australia which killed 35 adults and children and wounded 23 more. Within months, conservative Prime Minister John Howard pushed through Australia's National Firearms Agreement, based on recommendations that were made by National Committee on Violence in 1988. The NFA's provisions included:[45]

1. Banning automatic and semi-automatic rifles and shotguns;

2. Uniform stringent firearms licensing, with a requirement for a proven reason to own the gun;
3. Prohibition or cancellation of firearms license for violence or health reasons;
4. Waiting periods for firearm purchases;
5. Security and storage requirements;
6. Sales regulations;
7. Compulsory buybacks of banned weapons. By 2001, 659,940 newly prohibited guns were bought back at market value and destroyed. Another 68,727 were bought back and destroyed in 2003. Thousands more non-prohibited guns were voluntarily surrendered.

There was significant opposition to the NFA's passage, and even now, there are attempts to roll back some of its provisions. Australia has numerous rifle clubs and sport shooting associations, with hundreds of thousands of members. (Ironically, the National Rifle Association of Australia primarily supports competitive shooting, not political activity.) Passions ran so high in 1996 that Howard wore a bullet-proof vest to the first community meeting on the proposed measures. The U.S.'s NRA tried to influence the debate in Australia,[46] then used the NFA to stoke support and outrage amongst gun owners in the U.S.[47]

The gun stockpile has been reduced by a third since 1996.[48] The number of households owning guns has dropped by half.

Mass shootings, defined as those having 5 or more fatalities, have essentially been halted. In the 17 years prior to the NFA, there were 104 fatalities and 52 wounded in 13 mass shootings in Australia, which averaged one per year. Since the NFA, only one shooting (in 2014) has had 5 fatalities, including the gunman.

The firearm suicide and homicide rates had been declining before the NFA, but the rate of decline doubled after the NFA.[49] From 1979-1996, Australia had 3.6 firearm fatalities per 100,000 population. From 1997-2013, that rate dropped to 1.2 per 100,000. However, since the non-firearm suicide and homicide rates declined with an even greater magnitude, researchers said it was impossible to attribute the decline in firearm deaths solely to the change in gun laws. Researchers observe that there was no substitution of non-firearms methods for suicide and homicide, as the rates of the latter also declined. Without the impulsivity, immediacy – and identity, I would say – of guns, suicides and homicides declined. Australia, like the U.K., has a homicide rate $1/30^{th}$ of the U.S.'s.

It's possible that other changes in Australian society contributed to the overall decline, such as improved and faster trauma care for attempted suicide and homicide. I wonder though, if perhaps the restrictions of firearms and a change in the gun identity of Australia led to a decrease in overall aggressive and devaluing tendencies, thus reducing both firearm and non-firearm related suicides and homicides. Perhaps Australian identity changed, no longer wedded to the love of guns. The buyback seems particularly relevant to my eyes, though all provisions were powerful. The act of letting go of one's gun, a prized possession, cannot but change you. A nation letting go of the means of violence is all the more powerful and transformative.

It is estimated that 200 lives per year have been saved by the NFA, saving $500 million a year, paying for the cost of the buybacks and other provisions many times over, if a monetary value can be placed on a life Australia has had an awakening of identity and communal responsibility in the intervening years as well, apologizing for actions against the aboriginal peoples and paying reparations. This lends support to the idea of a changing Australian national identity, less tribalistic and self-centered, and more compassionate. I would suggest that Australia collectively decided to "do no harm to self or other" by enacting the NFA, and is living the fruits of that value to this day, in both firearm and non-firearm suicides and homicides.

John Howard looked back on his motivations to pass the NFA, and commented on American identity:

> "I did not want Australia to go down the American path. There are some things about America I admire, there are some things I

don't and one of the things I don't admire about America is an almost drooling, slavish love of guns. I think they're evil."[50]

Guns, race and identity in American culture

GUNS HAVE BEEN VALORIZED in American popular culture and imagination for over a century. The country was founded on armed revolution by citizen soldiers and militiamen; expansion into the frontier depended on gun hunting for subsistence and gun protection from wild predators; and settlers were encouraged to fight and kill Native Americans, hostile and otherwise. Though these goads to gun ownership largely faded by the 20th century, the archetype of the rugged individualist frontiersman, lone defender of hearth and home, persists to this day. In particular, the self-defense of Whites against presumably hostile non-Whites continues to be a trope used by politicians (think Willy Horton by George H.W. Bush, and Mexican "rapists and criminals" by Donald Trump) and Whites-at-large (Trayvon Martin and too many others). Gun identity and gun culture cannot be fully separated from racism. Even though violent crime has declined over the last three decades, fear of dark others still motivates. When racism overlaps with fears of governmental regulation, gun sales go through the roof. A vendor at a gun show stated that "President Obama was our biggest gun salesman,"[51] supposedly because of his attitudes towards gun control, but I can't help but think something more sinister was also at work. The Southern Poverty Law Center noted[52] a rise in the number of hate groups, peaking at 1018 the end of President Obama's first term, then dropping off only to rise again to 892 in 2015. Antigovernment extremist groups grew explosively. During all the Bush years, they numbered about 150. They skyrocketed to 1360 by 2012. In 2015, there were 998.

Richard Hofstadter wrote[53] in 1970's "America as a Gun Culture":

> (T)he most gun-addicted sections of the United States are the South and the Southwest. In 1968, when the House voted for a mild bill

to restrict the mail-order sale of rifles, shotguns, and ammunition, all but a few of the 118 votes against it came from these regions. This no doubt has something to do with the rural character of these regions, but it also stems from another consideration: in the historic system of the South, having a gun was a white prerogative. From the days of colonial slavery, when white indentured servants were permitted, and under some circumstances encouraged, to have guns, blacks, whether slave or free, were denied the right. **The gun, though it had a natural place in the South's outdoor culture, as well as a necessary place in the work of slave patrols, was also an important symbol of white male status.** (RC – emphasis mine.)

Moreover, gun ownership in the South is further stoked by distrust of government because of the Civil War, on top of national ambivalence about government dating back to the Revolution. First, Whites are given status and privilege ("identity") through historical racism. Guns become symbols of their status and privilege. Then identity is staked on the possession of guns. Finally, any attempt to regulate or "take away" guns is viewed as a threat to identity and "individualism." By suggesting a change in the way guns are handled by the culture, we are suggesting a change in White male identity itself. Of course, there are plenty of White males who believe in the necessity of these changes, as reflected in opinions of gun regulations. The majority of gun owners believe in commensense gun regulations, with support approaching the attitudes of non-gunowners.[54] But the NRA cabal and their allies seem particularly tied to White male and nativist ideology. Naturally, this is all cloaked in rationalizations involving the Constitution, freedom and liberty – but we should not allow ourselves to be gaslighted and misled.

Wayne LaPierre, CEO and executive vice president of the NRA, offered his typical full-throated proclamation and confirmation of the gun identity in a speech to CPAC (the Conservative Political Action Conference) one week after the Marjory Stoneman Douglas school shooting in Parkland, Florida. He accused his opposition of being "opportunists (who) exploit tragedy for political gain." No mention of the "opportunism" of himself and other gun identitarians in advancing pro-gun policies that week. He stoked fear of an imminent takeover of government by "European Socialists" and elites who "looked down" on the supposedly beleaguered, hardy and courageous gun owner, sole holder of 'true American values,'[55] chief among them, individualism itself - as if being an individual required gun ownership. Guns, in his view, elevate our selfhood.

> "We mourn the loss of the innocent... We share a goal of safe schools. But the opportunists wasted not one second to exploit tragedy for political gain. Saul Alinsky would have been proud. The break-back speed of calls for more gun control laws, and the breathless national media eager to smear the NRA. In the midst of genuine grief... what do we find? Chris Murphy, Nancy Pelosi and more eager to call for even more government control. They hate the NRA. They hate individual freedom. The elites care not one whit about America's school system. If they truly cared, they would protect them. For them, it's not a safety issue, it's a political issue. They care more about control and more of it. Their goal is to eliminate the

2nd Amendment and our firearms freedoms, so they can eradicate all individual freedoms. What they want is more restrictions on the law-abiding…Their solution is to make all of you less free." (Applause.)

Individualistic White male identity has historically been exemplified by gun ownership, but now LaPierre would have us believe that it is all individual freedom that's at stake. It's not culturally acceptable to talk directly to White male identity (although this has changed during Trump's tenure) – but apparently a gun can be used as a dog whistle. Who knew? (If guns could be reclassified as dog whistles, perhaps they would no longer be protected under the Second Amendment….hmmm. But then we'd have to agree racism is not in our national DNA anymore. Still working on that.)

There is no way to talk about the panic and paranoia around gun control without discussing White male anxieties about changing demographics, status, and unavoidable changes in masculine and individual identity as we move towards a more inclusive and responsible society. Vague (and not so vague) fears and resentments about these changes get crystallized for many into gun ownership and all forms of political backlash against those changes. There is fear of being left out, and fear of transformation. If an individualist mentality is part of his ethos, then there is a fear of intimacy, especially with those outside his tribe.* Resentment boils into blame: blame of the government which he thinks is forcing this change, and blame of anyone who might be subtly implying that part of his identity (his affinity for guns, his version of "masculinity," his racism) might be at least partially responsible for the problems we face. Instead of accepting responsibility, a certain kind of White male falls to narcissistic, self-centered defenses, losing empathy and devaluing others. It is his power complex, aimed at defeating and warding off a changing world.

He adamantly claims his gun is for protection, but guns rarely protect. As mentioned previously,

---

* But perhaps intimacy is difficult anyway for this group: white males, particularly older white males, are at higher risk for depression, loneliness and suicide – partly because they own more guns, and partly because of a paucity of relationships.

less than 1% of gun homicides were committed in self-defense, and a similarly small percentage were cited as having been used to resist potential attackers.[56] Similarly, gun carrying is a paradoxical experience for juvenile offenders. Loughran *et al* looked[57] at over 1200 adolescent offenders. Gun carriers perceived lower risks associated with offending when carrying guns, and higher reward. However, guns were actually associated with higher risks of violence.

I've primarily written about White male identity and gun identity – as mentioned, almost 50% of White men own guns. But we must face other aspects of being male. In our culture, men are not given space to talk about their vulnerability, depression, anxieties, insecurities, loneliness, and isolation. Instead of relating to others about these vulnerabilities, they are more prone to turning to substances, and reacting to vulnerability in anger and hostility. I wrote about Asian American male (and female) anger and domestic violence in *Asian American Anger: It's a Thing!* (Available for free download at www.RaviChandraMD.com and for

Kindle and iBooks.) Men need compassion, and need to cultivate compassion, allowing the feminine principle of relatedness to help them become whole and at peace. As men, we also need to examine how gender roles, masculinity and toxic masculinity, entitlement to power and patriarchy distort who we are and can be. As I wrote in *Asian American Anger*:

> "This 'world-defining relationship' of men and women, marred in the extreme by violence, is prime evidence of the world's brokenness and suffering. It is also, by nature, the main hope for the world's redemption, which must, of course, be in the triumph of love. If there is a gender war, there are many more gender collaborators. We are, after all, not entrenched enemies. We're mothers and fathers, brothers and sisters, partners, friends. Community.
>
> With, one hopes, a mutual, common destiny."

Buying a gun means buying into an identity, an ideology, a psychological defense more than buying into an actual physical defense. The material defense is often mainly a cover for the psyche's gravitation towards aggression and defense against corporeal and philosophical threat, man against man, and usually, in this country, White against non-White. Guns become more important than facts. Guns create their own "facts." Gun identitarians machine-gun bullet-point, self-rationalizing arguments to justify the status of their true love. Guns have their own Archimedes' principle, displacing an equivalent mass of empathy and compassion. Our humanity splashes out of the tub.

Identity, guns and transcendence

WHAT IS IDENTITY? SOME would say it's a social category one identifies with or is placed in. I take a more personal view. I would define identity as an experience of selfhood based on relationship to one's own personal attributes (race, gender, class, nationality, regionality, religous affiliation, etc.); one's body, speech, activities, memories and history in life; one's mind, thoughts and emotions, including desires, fantasies, wishes and fears; one's philosophical or religious framework and values; other people, namely one's family and friends, non-friends and enemies; one's community, state, nation and world; geographical and environmental influences; other living beings as a whole; and even one's possessions. It is an experience of being a "one." It is both an exterior and interior phenomenon. In medical terms, identity is a bio/psycho/socio/cultural/spiritual experience. This experience may be coherent or incoherent, consistent or inconsistent over time, and variable depending on situational and relational factors. As Walt Whitman proclaimed, "I am large, I contain multitudes." Psychiatrists and other mental health professionals often speak of the self as being composed of many interdependent and sometimes practically independently functioning parts.

A Collection of Parts
April, 2013

I am a collection of parts, a multitude of selves –
They play inside me like precocious elves.
A warrior battles, a peacemaker works

A heart/mind bureau, with tireless clerks.
A woman, a child, an adversary, a friend –
Critics and supporters and actors with ends.
Healer and patient, trickster and mole
They observe, they comment,
they sometimes control.
An emergence, a symphony, a chorus, a blend -
A circus I carry, a circle I mend.
Admirers with whispers, detractors with swords
This collection is work – I'm never bored.
Fractious and playful, serious and fun,
Interdependent we are, from many we're one.

From a Buddhist standpoint, identity is more of an event than an entity. It is more flexible and nuanced, less attached and suffused with compassion, striving to view the world from multiple perspectives rather than being stuck in one. It is confluent with and strives for peace with all, rather than fixed, defensive and rigid against other identities. Buddhists hold that belief in and attachment to the concept that the self exists independently is the root of suffering. When we think of ourselves as independently existing, we get caught up in greed, hatred and jealousy to supply and defend our isolated self. This self-centeredness causes suffering to ourselves and others. Enlightenment is the insight and experience of interdependent existence. From an enlightened, interdependent perspective, we can feel connected and beyond difficult emotions. Belonging is the opposite of suffering.

> "What did the Buddhist say to the hot dog vendor?"
>
> "Make me one with everything!"

Developmentally, human beings need connection, affection, attachment and nurturing to thrive. These could conceivably help lead to those experiences of oneness, belonging and overcoming of suffering. According to self psychology, when there is empathic failure, the self feels in danger of disintegration and fragmentation. It reaches for stabilizing objects, which may be people, possessions or principles. These stabilizing objects "fill a 'hole' in the self, stabilizing the self structure and preventing further fragmentation. As a result of this process the disintegration anxiety is controlled."[58]

Feldmann and Johnson continue, in their 1992 paper on the psychological function of weapons:

> "How might weapons function as selfobjects? They may provide a sense of power, omnipotence, and mastery for the damaged self. Weapons may also allow the self to feel in control. They may serve as a source of stimulation and excitement for the empty self. By providing these things the self feels more effective; in essence this is an empathic response from the weapon. The weapon not only allows the self to feel in control of situations and its own cohesion, by their very nature they allow the self to feel control over the selfobject (analogous to a merger transference); because the merger transference is a more primitive type of selfobject transference, this may imply that the use of weapons as selfobjects is also a more primitive and pathological process."

(A 'transference' was originally defined as the redirection of childhood emotions towards caregivers onto a therapist or other object. Nowadays it refers simply to all emotions felt towards that other. A *merger transference* implies a loss of boundary with the weapon, in this case, so that the weapon and self are one and idealized, and one thinks one has control, when in fact one may be surrendering control to the weapon. This seems different than the attenuation of boundaries in Buddhism, which is more generalized and associated with growth, maturation and reduction of difficult emotions - a realization of the self as not inherently existing, but rather interdependently existing. The pathological attachment to a weapon is a dependence, using the weapon to fend off disintegration of the self.)

John Hinckley, who tried to assassinate President Ronald Reagan in 1981 gives a prime example of the selfobject function of guns. He wrote a poem entitled "Guns Are Fun," quoted by Feldmann and Johnson, which includes these lines:

> "This gun gives me pornographic power…
> and the world will look at me in disbelief,
> all because I own this inexpensive gun…
> Guns are loveable.
> Guns are fun.
> Are you lucky enough to own one?"

It could be an advertising jingle.

Feldmann and Johnson also cite Mark Chapman (who murdered John Lennon) and Travis Bickle. (Bickle is the fictional character in *Taxi Driver* who inspired Hinckley – who was also inspired by Chapman, by the way. Violence is contagious, each act inspiring another, if conditions permit.)

> "For Mark Chapman, John Hinckley, and Travis Bickle, preoccupation with weapons follows an empathic failure on the part of a significant selfobject."

Certainly, most shooters are resentful, aggrieved victim-perpetrators, angry at a target who has injured them emotionally. But this analysis goes farther than that. They also think their weapon makes them whole and powerful again, and thus merge with it. For Chapman, Hinckley, Bickle, men like them and gun identitarians, guns provide the empathy, coherence, cohesion and validation they feel lacking in society. If society empathized with them, it would protect them. Not only won't society protect them, it menaces them. What society won't do, the gun will.

I take the opposite perspective. A society composed of responsible individuals functioning under the rule of law does protect me, and has sufficient empathy to sustain me. Guns are the menace to me, not society. However, our society of late does seem to offer more menace than empathy, with a president who threatens, blames and devalues everyone who disagrees with him, and those whose solution to school shootings is armed teachers. I obviously want a more just, empathic and compassionate society, but I see that this can only happen when we choose closer relations with each other, not closer relation with weapons.

In the absence of close relations, weapons proliferate, substituting for relations with people and creating a vicious cycle of decreasing security and empathic failures so large they could swallow 17 in Parkland, 49 at the Pulse Nightclub, 58 In Las Vegas, 26 at Sandy Hook, and thousands more in the workaday violence that barely makes headlines. Empathic failures lead to an attachment to guns and also to a self-centered, narcissistic gun identity which grandiosely exalts the man-with-his-gun, and devalues all others.

"Come and Take It," reads the bumper sticker on a pickup truck, above the image of an AR-15, and next to an NRA decal. The implication is clear: you'd "take" a round of bullets if you dared try to take his gun. "This gun is more important to me than your life." It's an expression of the ultimate combination of gun idealization, gun identity and merger, the tribal, totemic power of the gun, and narcissistic if not sociopathic stance of a macho, stoic tough-guy gun owner. It's not exactly a bumper sticker that declares openness to conversation, and neither is he. He is Dirty Harry with an AR-15 and a pickup truck, declaring his love and attachment for the one thing he can count on. He's a defender of individual liberty with the gun. Who would he be without it? I wonder if he ever thinks about this question.

We even get attached to gun identity in play, which leads people to oppose gun control. Video gaming has been associated with increased aggression, decreased empathy, and more tolerance for sexual harassment. Lapierre and Farrar found[59] that gaming, particularly use of realistic gun controllers in first-person shooters was correlated with more negative attitudes toward gun control and positive attitudes towards gun availability, even after controlling for variables such as libertarian beliefs. It's hard to know if this is causal or simply a correlation, but it's possible that video game exposure is influencing gun culture and attitudes in the real world.

We all get attached to objects and people, and it's almost always not pathological. Some attachments, like parent and child, are essential for life. Smartphones and social media, less so, as laid out in my book *Facebuddha: Transcendence in the Age of Social Networks*. But shouldn't we be curious about the nature of our attachments, rather than doubling down on them? Shouldn't we wonder what they're doing to our hearts and minds, relationship and environment? That wondering would be the mark of a true *individual*, in my book. The gun identity bypasses that curiosity. The gun identitarian would no more question his gun than his liver.

I could not find much research on the personalities of gun owners, probably because it's not easily funded. (In 1996, the CDC was effectively barred by Congress from conducting research that might support gun control.)[60] A small study of self-selected gun owners in the 1970s revealed no atypical personality characteristics when compared with gun nonowners or national norms. However, the survey also indicated they had lower sociability and higher need for power than gun nonowners.[61] Gun owners were not more insecure than gun nonowners. (But obviously, the study couldn't assess their insecurity if their guns were taken away. Also, since the subjects volunteered, the results are not generalizable to the population of all gun owners.) In another study, gun ownership was positively correlated with antisocial behavior across the board amongst middle schoolers, but some gun owners were much higher risk than others, suggesting that targeted public health interventions could help. A survey of over 6000 primarily Black rural and non-metropolitan students revealed that those who owned guns in order to gain respect or frighten others also reported extremely high rates of antisocial behavior. Those who owned guns for sporting reasons reported rates of antisocial behavior only slightly higher than those reported by youth who did not own guns.[62] Shapiro *et al* administered the Attitudes Towards Guns and Violence Questionnaire (AGVQ) to 1619 students in grades 3-7 and 9, 11 and 12 in the mid-1990s.[63] They found that self-reported gun owners rated 1.5 standard deviations higher on four factors: aggressive response to shame, comfort with aggression, excitement and power/safety. These are all favorable attitudes towards violence; without them, one is unlikely to want to own a gun. They note that "the desire to own a gun does not seem to occur as a discrete, separate attitude but instead seems largely a function of general attitudes concerning interpersonal conflict and agggression." It's unclear how the general population of gun owners would compare; but clearly these are concerning predispositions towards aggression. Anecdotally, we can recall the target manufacturers who sold boy-in-a-hoodie targets after the Trayvon Martin shooting, and draw our own conclusions about the attitudes of gun owners towards aggression. But research would be helpful.

Another recent study actually did look at target-shooters.[54] (The study was done in Germany because several mass shootings there involved youth who'd been involved in shooting clubs.) Target-shooters but not basketball players had higher aggression and anxiety scores after team practice. A one-year longitudinal study showed that target-shooters' initial self-reported aggression was higher and increased after a year. They also showed deficient emotional-regulation strategies, and this was correlated with self-reported aggression. However, their self-concept became more peaceful, indicating some discrepancy. (This may be due to how certain items were interpreted, such as feeling safer with a gun, therefore more peaceful.) The authors suggest that American target-shooters might be even more aggressive, due to differences in the culture of target shooting and gun regulation in general. Hunters, though, are not reported to rate higher on aggression. Other than studies like these few, I'm largely left with my own impressions, which are in danger of being stereotypes. We need more research, clearly, but there is at least a suggestion that owning and using guns changes one's personality. What you do, what you own, and whom you know changes you. Gun owners may be changing in all of these ways.

Berkowitz and LePage coined the term "weapons effect" in 1967. They found that the mere presence of a weapon led to more aggressive responses in individuals presented with a painful stimulus.[65] This effect has been replicated by numerous researchers. Other recent studies show that reading times for aggressive words was faster when paired with weapon-related words rather than animal- or nature-related words. These types of results seem to be stronger for boys than girls. Another study showed that those with concealed weapons in their cars drove more aggressively than those without weapons, even after controlling for factors such as gender, age, urbanization, census region and driving frequency. As Berkowitz noted, "Guns not only permit violence, they can stimulate it as well. The finger pulls the trigger, but the trigger may also be pulling the finger."[66] You don't control the weapon; the weapon controls you, giving you thoughts, emotions, predisposition to actions – and a new identity.

Carter *et al* surveyed youth injured in assault.[67] They found

> "Participants with firearms were noted to have more aggressive attitudes compared to those without firearms, suggesting aggressive attitudes and subsequent retaliation are major contributors to violent firearm-related injury. ED studies have shown that assault-related injuries among youth are often the result of long-standing disagreements and that retaliation may be an underlying cause for violence. These findings are important because health behavior models, which are key to many violence-prevention efforts, suggest the first step to decreasing future aggression would be to modify aggressive attitudes."

Opposition to gun control is significantly stronger in Whites than Blacks, and racism is a powerful correlate of gun ownership and attitudes towards gun control. Filindra and Kaplan concluded "racial resentment is a statistically significant and substantively important predictor of white opposition to gun control." Subjects who were primed with images of Blacks from the Implicit Association Test were more opposed to gun control than a control group.[68]" O'Brien *et al* studied a large sample in the American National Election Study.[69] They found that symbolic racism (implicit bias and racial resentment) was related to having a gun in the home and opposition to gun control policies. This relationship was maintained even controlling for "conservative ideologies, political affiliation, opposition to government control, and being from a southern state, which are otherwise strong predictors of gun ownership and opposition to gun reform." These authors note that it's possible that gun ownership leads to more racist attitudes, rising alongside other indicators of aggression, like salivary cortisol. Either way, it's not a good look on you, America.

Stroebe *et al* found "Belief in a Dangerous World" (BDW) is a predictor of gun ownership in their recent survey of over 800 U.S. males.[70] BDW has been correlated with negative attitudes towards minorities, and encompasses paranoia about the government and fears of imminent social collapse as well. Objective risk of assault was not a good predictor of gun ownership. How to address this toxic belief, underpinned with racism? Beliefs and worldviews are part of identity, and BDW also represents an empathic failure. These believers are right about the existential vulnerability of being human, but they are fundamentally less trustful and more menaced by others, propelling them into a gun identity. Instead of responding to their vulnerability with compassion, they react defensively, patching the "hole" with a gun, activating a love of power that substitutes for love of fellow man. It's a process of devaluation, which distorts the gun owner as well. Like survivalists, they harden themselves against the collapse of the world, instead of supporting civic institutions that would build a safer, saner society.

As I write these words, I feel that I may be in danger of dehumanizing the gun owner. At the same time, from what I can see in bumper stickers and public statements, many gun owners see their guns as completing their humanity, their Americanity, and *ipso facto*, they would feel less human without them, less American. No wonder the NRA pushes for concealed carry nationwide. No wonder many gun owners react so strongly against gun control (even though a majority of them still favor common sense gun regulation.)[71] Furthermore, the presence of so many guns automatically produces insecurity, vulnerability and threat of death to all of us. So it is we who are being threatened and dehumanized by the presence of guns. Guns (as currently regulated in the culture) are a grandiosity to their owner, and a devaluation of others – the classic narcissistic and sociopathic defense. When I get trolled on social media and on Amazon for writing this essay, it will only prove the relationship.

Weapons have served various purposes in cultures throughout human history. Sikhs are supposed to carry a kirpan, a ceremonial dagger, as an article of faith. Christ declares in Matthew that he "has not come to bring peace, but a sword." We speak of a "sword of justice," which originally was a monarch's supreme judicial power. Many cultures have given men or sometimes women weapons to mark coming of age. Feldmann and Johnson cite examples such as the Zulu, for whom weapons were symbols of power; the Copper Eskimos, where decorated weapons represented creativity and hunting prowess; the Jivaro of South America, whose elaborate blowguns conferred prestige; and the Plains Indians of North America, for whom horses and guns conferred status and proved skill.

My friend, a White male psychiatrist in his mid-70s who grew up in the far northern reaches of California, said at his father's eulogy, "my father taught me to ride a horse, drive a car, and shoot a gun." The gun was casually and yet vitally a part of his coming of age and relation to his father, whose love and protection was transferred through the gun itself. They are now nostalgic reminders of his father, his childrens' grandfather. I imagine many men (and women) like this, with guns the family pastime and heirloom. No wonder they become markers of identity and culture. If your family is a gun family, you are more likely to want guns. Indeed, researchers found that 1st and 2nd graders who reported real or toy guns at home were more likely to think they would own real guns in the future.[72]

But we can't accept these markers of identity casually, and not question their pathology. Cukier *et al* quote Katz's "Advertising and the construction of violent white masculinity":

> "'Guns are an important signifier of virility and power and hence an important way violent masculinity is constructed and then sold to audiences. In fact, the presence of guns in magazine and newspaper ads is crucial to communicating the extent of a movie's violent content . . . images of gun-toting macho males pervade the visual landscape.' These stereotypes are particularly strong among disempowered white working-class men."

Nuclear weapons are our most destructive pastimes and heirlooms, symbols of intellectual, cultural and military power. The differences between primitive weapons, guns and nuclear weapons are clear, but they all share a sheer capacity to end life, even all life on earth. While their proponents say that they are in fact used to save the life of the tribe, their potential engages the nihilistic death wish of a culture. We should wonder whether our American culture is expressing an extraordinary wish to destroy itself, expressed in its strident, bizarre attachments to guns. If it is in a process of destruction, what would the proponents of guns create from its ashes? Do they have a goal at all, or is their pursuit heedless of consequence, useful primarily to instill fear and anguish in their "enemies?" That is in itself a form of destruction and declaration of nihilistic power.

Perhaps nuclear weapons offer an example of an alternative way of thinking about weapons and power. Not using them, or even denuclearizing, represents wisdom, compassion and the power of restraint to most of us. Perhaps the only good weapon is a sheathed, unsharpened, or even destroyed weapon. One that has been let go of and given up, restoring safety and humanity to all, as our consciousness evolves beyond the wish to kill, and turns to the wish to save and help. To live, and help others live.

If we can transcend the gun identity, we can transcend identity itself. In this transcendence, we will find our truest belonging.

Conclusions

"MANY OTHERWISE INTELLIGENT AMERICANS cling with pathetic stubbornness to the notion that the people's right to bear arms is the greatest protection of their individual rights and a firm safeguard of democracy—without being in the slightest perturbed by the fact that no other democracy in the world observes any such 'right' and that in some democracies in which citizens' rights are rather better protected than in ours, such as England and the Scandinavian countries, our arms control policies would be considered laughable."

— Richard Hofstadter, 1970

The First Amendment right to speech is not absolute, and is weighed against harms that speech could cause. It seems reasonable to weigh any right to bear arms, whether for self-defense or as member of a militia, against the harms (suicide, homicide and perhaps even the mental health effects of the presence of so many weapons) that result from an inadequately regulated individual right. So far, we've struggled with doing so because of our nation's gun identity, embodied and emboldened by the NRA and their allies. Many gun owners are easily panicked about the loss of Second Amendment rights, all individual freedoms, the encroachment of government, and general societal collapse. A substantial number of Whites harbor negative attitudes towards people of color, as well as a gun identity, and seem to fear changing demographics, from immigration to increasing diversity. But these changes are inevitable. Because they are inevitable, they trigger the survival-brain's fight mechanism in those predisposed, viscerally linked to their gun identity, hostility towards others and a rabid defense of the Second Amendment as they wish to read it.

Never having had my aforementiond friend's paternal connection to guns, where guns were a rite of passage to both his father's approval and manhood, this is my sense of the situation, in SAT form:

Guns : Me :: Undocumented immigrants : Nativists

For me, guns are these strange alien objects which do not belong in my house. I have to work to understand why others need them and want to protect them so badly. The difference, of course, is that immigrants are people; guns are not. But somehow, guns have been accorded more humanity than people by the gun fetishist. One man lovingly spoke of his AR-15: "that's my baby."[73] Perhaps guns fortify the gun owner's sense of his own humanity and identity. Or perhaps they are totems of a higher power. They become almost gods themselves.

My high school classmate in Michigan had a bumper sticker: "God, Guns and Ammo!" The three are interchangeable avatars, synonymous to the gun identititarian. Are Guns and Ammo America's God? Or will we choose a different source of light than the blazing barrels of our rifles? For now, it appears we worship guns more than we worship the teachings of Christ, Buddha, the Torah, Quran or any other pretender to the throne. Perhaps the latter matter least in our American equation. It's primarily Christ who has been supplanted here; or perhaps Christian gun enthusiasts see Jesus with a .357 Magnum instead of cradling a lamb. ("Maybe he shot the lamb, right? You never know.")

There are surely more guns and bullets than bibles existent in the U.S. today. You might say there are more coffee cups too, but we can easily see the difference in regard. In fact, there are more gun retail shops in the U.S. than there are Starbucks in the entire world. The idol of our age is not the golden calf; it is the AR-15, the Glock 17 pistol, the bump stock, the Ruger 10/22 rifle, the Mossberg 930 semi-automatic, the Kel-Tec PMR-30 revolver. The Remington, the Smith & Wesson, the Colt – are our Saints. We season them with rounds "like…a frying pan"[74] preparing for our religion's true communion meal, ascension and sacrament: killing our enemy. In Cold Blood We Trust. We value guns more than we value the lives of our little ones, our angels, our children, our neighbors, our fellow travelers on this blue Earth. If this isn't a sickness, I don't know what is.

The NRA has an annual budget of over $250 million.[75] Between 2000 and 2010, the NRA spent 15 times more than gun control organizations on polical campaigns. It spent $11.4 million on President Trump's presidential campaign, plus another $20 million attacking Hillary Clinton.[76] They spent $34.5 million campaigning against Democrats, and $14.5 million supporting Republicans. In 2017, they spent almost $5 million lobbying Congress. Between 1998 and 2017, the NRA spent $203.2 million on direct political activities, according to Politifact.[77] There's no stronger identity than one backed by wealth and power. The NRA's deep pockets are our deep state, and their most potent weapon. In our current political environment, we will have to outspend them to beat them, and that still might not be enough, because the gun identity is so deeply lodged in the American psyche. But perhaps beating the NRA would be the first step at dislodging the gun identity. There are some positive signs in March, 2018. Over a dozen companies have severed ties with the NRA, now refusing to give NRA members discounts and other perks. Also breaking with the NRA, Walmart and Dick's Sporting Goods have significantly shifted their policies on gun sales: both raised the minimum age to buy guns to 21, regardless of local laws, and the latter ceased sales of assault-type rifles like the AR-15.

But it's not just the NRA. The Pew Center reported gun enthusiasts were almost twice as likely to contact their representatives about gun rights than gun nonowners.[78] Gun owners have been more vocal than those who support gun control measures.

During a 2016 campaign rally, Donald Trump listed presumed threats of a Hillary Clinton presidency, at least one of them quite false, that she planned to eliminate the Second Amendment. He continued, "if she gets to pick – if she gets to pick her judges, nothing you can do, folks. Although the Second Amendment people, maybe there is, I don't know." He later claimed he was suggesting political organization, not assassination, but it was clearly open to interpretation. Either way, a gun identity is linked to Republican and even 'true' American identity. The day after meeting with survivors of Parkland, Trump tweeted support of the NRA:[79]

> "What many people don't understand, or don't want to understand, is that Wayne, Chris and the folks who work so hard at the @NRA are Great People and Great American Patriots. They love our Country and will do the right thing. MAKE AMERICA GREAT AGAIN!"

Trump initially favored NRA-supported "hardened schools." "Highly trained teachers would also serve as a deterrent to the cowards that do this. ATTACKS WOULD END!" he tweeted.

Later, he appeared to reverse himself. Before reversing himself again, appearing to support a long-stalled bipartisan effort in the Senate. Before reversing himself again and saying he was "against gun control," after meeting with NRA representatives. Donald Trump has done more 1080's on gun control than Chloe Kim winning gold on the snowboard halfpipe.

If Nixon went to China, perhaps Trump can go to the NRA and his gun-identitarian base. I am not hopeful, but I would like to be proven wrong. This is an issue that transcends party affiliation; transcends race, class and gender. In order to get it right, we will have to transcend identity, to find new relationship and new belonging as Americans.

The gun identity is grounded in fears, and tied to a certain kind of masculinity and devaluation of the lives of others. Gun identity represents a narcissistic, and at times even a sociopathic, extreme. What would happen if we brought compassion to our underlying insecurity, vulnerabilty and fear – instead of trying to escape them with a fixation on guns? Our fix of ammo? "Give us this day our daily ammunition." We will transcend the gun identity when we decide that the power to kill is not the power we crave; but rather the strength to love, the power to prevent harm, the will to live and help others live.

We don't need teachers armed with guns. We need citizens armed with questions. We don't need an NRA encouraging gun sales by arming us with fear of our fellow man. We need legislators armed with concern for the public good, and policies to turn concern into action. We don't need narcissism to rule us. We need benevolence, trust, humility and common humanity. We don't need the LaPierre's and Trump's fixing blame on others. We need people of all races, ethnicities and regions taking responsibility for creating a safer nation. We don't need more "good guys with guns." We need fewer guns. We need to disarm our gun-crazed American identity.

***

The steel of a gun is the coldest thing in the world. Even when silent it shouts a threat. But it has never been silent, never in the history of the United States.

But there are other voices. There are the screams of millions dead. More have died by gunshot than in all our country's wars combined. Are these millions louder than the gun?

Only if we join their cry. We must speak for the dead. We must speak for the living. We must speak, or be silenced by death itself, seeping out of the barrels of our guns, 350 million and counting.

Ravi Chandra, M.D.
March 1, 2018
San Francisco, California

Postscript

Just as this manuscript was going to press, Florida Governor Rick Scott signed into law the Marjory Stoneman Douglas High School Public Safety Act, the first significant gun control legislation in the state in 20 years. Predictably, the NRA has reflexively filed suit to block this measure. The act falls far short of the public health measures proposed by experts, and even further short of disarming our gun identity. We need much more, across the entire country. Nothing short of transforming who we are as a nation, who we are to each other, will be enough.

Gun Attitude Scale

THE GUN ATTITUDE SCALE (GAS) was developed by Tenhundfeld *et al.*[80] Dr. Tenhundfeld is currently at the U.S. Air Force Academy, and this scale was reprinted with his permission. The GAS has 20 items which are scored on a 4-point Likert scale from "agree strongly" to "disagree strongly." The questions serve as a useful assessment of attitudes towards guns, and will hopefully be used in future research. Clearly, changing these attitudes and others is vital if we are to change policy and have a safer country. Understanding these attitudes and what gives rise to them is an important step.

1. A gun in the home is more likely to shoot a household member than an intruder
2. I would personally feel safer by owning a gun

3. I would personally feel more in control by keeping a gun in my home
4. I would not hesitate to shoot an attacker on the street
5. I would not hesitate to shoot an intruder who breaks into my home
6. Owning a gun would give me a feeling of independence
7. Owning a gun would help me to protect my home and property
8. Handguns in the home cause too many accidental shootings
9. I support the right to own a firearm
10. I support the right to carry a firearm outside of the home
11. I am concerned about losing my second amendment right to own a gun
12. I would enjoy sport shooting
13. I would be interested in taking a self-defense course that included hand gun training
14. I would personally feel more powerful by carrying/keeping a handgun

15. I am confident that I could successfully defend myself using a handgun
16. A gun in the home is more likely to lead to the suicide of a family member than to protect family members
17. I am afraid of guns
18. Hunting with guns is a sport I am likely to enjoy
19. All guns stored at home should be locked in a safe
20. I enjoy hunting with guns but I would never use a gun on another person

Endnotes

1. Cukier W, Eagen SA. Gun violence. Curr Opin Psychology 2018, 19:109-112
2. BBC News. America's gun culture in 10 charts. http://www.bbc.com/news/world-us-canada-41488081 accessed 3/1/18
3. Parker K, Horowitz JM, Igielnik R, Oliphant B, Brown A. America's complex relationship with guns: an in-depth look at the attitudes and experiences of U.S. adults. Pew Research Center. June 22, 2017. http://www.pewsocialtrends.org/2017/06/22/americas-complex-relationship-with-guns/ accessed 2/27/18 and Igielnik R, Brown A. Key takeaways on Americans' views of guns and gun ownership. Pew Research Center. June 22, 2017. http://www.pewresearch.org/fact-tank/2017/06/22/key-takeaways-on-americans-views-of-guns-and-gun-ownership/ accessed 2/27/18
4. Christoffel KK, Naureckas SM. Firearm injuries in children and adolescents: epidemiology and preventive approaches. Curr Opin Pediatr 1994; 6:519-524
5. Betz ME, Barber C, Miller M. Suicidal behavior and firearm access: results from the second injury control and risk survey. Suicide Life Threat Behav 2011 Aug;41(4):384-391

6. Anglemyer A, Horvath T, Rutherford G. The accessibility of firearms and risk for suicide and homicide victimization among household members: a systematic review and meta-analysis. Ann Int Med 2014; 160:101-110
7. Christoffel KK, Naureckas SM. *op. cit.*
8. Kellerman AL, Rivara FP, Rushforth NB et al. Gun ownership as a risk factor for homicide in the home. NEJM 1993; 329:1084-1091 http://www.nejm.org/doi/full/10.1056/NEJM199310073291506 accessed 2/24/18
9. Coyne-Beasley T, Baccaglini L, Johnson RM, Webster B, Wiebe DJ. Do partners with children know about firearms in their home? Evidence of a gender gap and implications for practitioners. Pediatrics 2005 2215(6):e662-e667
10. Stroebe W, Leander NP, Kruglanski AW. Is it a dangerous world out there? The motivational bases of American gun ownership. Pers and Soc Psych Bull. 2017, 43(8):1071-1085
11. Cited in Byrdsong TR, Devan A, Yamatani H. A ground-up model for gun violence reduction: a community-based public health approach. J Evid Inf Soc Work 2016;13(1):76-86
12. Carter PM, Walton MA, Newton MF et al. Firearm possession among adolescents presenting to an urban emergency department for assault. Pediatrics 2013; 132(2):213-221
13. Kristof N. How to reduce shootings. New York Times, updated February 20, 2018. https://www.nytimes.com/interactive/2017/11/06/opinion/how-to-reduce-shootings.html accessed 2/19/18

14. Anestis MD, Anestis JC, Butterworth SE. Handgun legislation and changes in statewide overall suicide rates. Am J Public Health. 2017;107:579-581
15. Kposowa A, Hamilton D, Want K. Impact of firearm availability and gun regulation on state suicide rates. Suicide Life Threat Behav. 2016 Dec;46(6):678-696
16. Fleegler EW, Lee LK, Monuteaux MC, Hemenway D, Mannix R. Firearm legislation and firearm-related fatalities in the United States. JAMA Intern Med. 2013;173(9):732-740
17. Kalesan B, Mobily ME, Keiser O, Fagan JA, Galea S. Firearm legislation and firearm mortality in the USA: a cross-sectional, state-level study. Lancet 2016;387:1847-55
18. Ladapo JA, Elliott MN, Kanouse DE, et al. Firearm ownership and acquisition among parents with risk factors for self-harm or other violence. Acad Pediatrics 2016;16:742-749
19. Green B, Horel T, Papachristos AV. Modeling contagion through social networks to explain and predict gunshot violence in Chicago, 2006 to 2014. JAMA Intern Med. 2017;177(3)326-333
20. Meindl JN, Ivy JW. Mass shootings: the role of the media in promoting generalized imitation. Am J Pub Health. 2017;107:368-370 doi:10.2105/AJPH.2016.303611
21. America's frontline physicians call on government to act on the public health epidemic of gun violence. February 16, 2018 https://www.psychiatry.org/newsroom/news-releases/america-s-frontline-physicians-call-on-government-to-act-on-the-

public-health-epidemic-of-gun-violence accessed 2/28/18

22. Bennett DJ, Ogloff JRP, Mullen PE, et al. Schizophrenia disorders, substance abuse and prior offending in a sequential series of 435 homicides. Acta Psychiatr Scand 2011 124: 226-233

23. Elbogen EB, Johnson SC. The intricate link between violence and mental disorder: results from the National Epidemiologic Survey on Alcohol and Related Conditions. Arch Gen Psychiatry 2009 Feb; 66(2):152-61

24. Swanson JW, McGinty EE, Fazel S, Mays VM. Mental illness and reduction of gun violence and suicide: bringing epidemiologic research to policy. Ann Epidemiol 2015 May;25(5)366-76

25. Swanson *et al, op. cit.*

26. Choe JY, Teplin LA, Abram KM. Perpetration of Violence, violent victimization, and severe mental illness: balancing public health concerns. Psychiatr Serv. 2008 February; 59(2): 153-164

27. Appelbaum PS. Violence and mental disorders: data and public policy. Am J Psychiatry 2006; 163: 1319-1321

28. Everytown for Gun Safety. Analysis of mass shootings. 2015 https://everytownresearch.org/documents/2015/09/analysis-mass-shootings.pdf accessed 2/27/18

29. Metzl J, MacLeish KT. Mass murders, mental illness and the politics of American firearms. Am J Public Health 2015; 105: 240-249

30. Carey B. Opening mental hospitals unlikely to prevent mass shootings, experts say. New York

Times, February 22, 2018 https://www.nytimes.com/2018/02/22/health/trump-mental-hospitals-parkland.html accessed 2/22/18

31. Lee BX, Lifton RJ, Sheehy G, *et al*. The dangerous case of Donald Trump: 27 psychiatrists and mental health experts assess a president. Thomas Dunne Books, 2017
32. Swanson *et al*, *op. cit*.
33. Lewiecki EM, Miller SA. Suicide, guns, and public policy. Am J Public Health 2013; 103: 27-31
34. Metzl J, MacLeish KT. *op. cit*.
35. Bangalore S, Messerli FH. Gun ownership and firearm-related deaths. Am J Med. 2013 Oct;126(10):873-876
36. Swanson *et al*, *op. cit*.
37. Waugaman E. Understanding America's obsession with guns: how did we get where we are? Psychoanalytic Inquiry. 2016;36(6):440-453
38. Parsons C. Trump 'supportive' of tougher gun law, but his record suggests that may not mean much. Los Angeles Times, February 20, 2018 http://www.latimes.com/politics/la-na-pol-trump-gun-history-20180220-story.html accessed 2/20/18
39. Sit R. Guns aren't responsible for school shootings, blame music and video games: Republican governor. Newsweek, 2/16/18 http://www.newsweek.com/parkland-school-shooting-second-amendment-gun-control-video-games-movies-nra-809681 accessed 2/20/18
40. Morgan CF. Congressman from North Carolina says America does not have a gun problem. WFMY News 2, February 19, 2018. http://www.

wfmynews2.com/sports/local/congressman-from-north-carolina-says-america-does-not-have-gun-problem/520709210, accessed 2/20/18

41. Hellman J. Congressional candidate defends AR-15 giveaway after school shooting. The Hill, Feb 19, 2018. http://thehill.com/homenews/campaign/374548-congressional-candidate-defends-giveaway-of-rifle-after-school-shooting accessed 2/20/18

42. Grynbaum M. Right-wing media uses Parkland shooting as conspiracy fodder. New York Times, February 20, 2018 https://www.nytimes.com/2018/02/20/business/media/parkland-shooting-media-conspiracy.html accessed 2/20/18

43. Scher B. Why the NRA always wins. Politico, February 19, 2018 https://www.politico.com/magazine/story/2018/02/19/why-the-nra-always-wins-217028 accessed 2/21/18

44. Dunblane massacre. Wikipedia online. https://en.wikipedia.org/wiki/Dunblane_massacre accessed 2/21/18

45. Dudley M, Rosen A, Alpers P, Peters R. The Port Arthur massacre and the National Firearms Agreement: 20 years on, what are the lessons? Med J Aust June, 2016 204(10):381-383

46. Port Arthur massacre: community and government reaction. Wikipedia https://en.wikipedia.org/wiki/Port_Arthur_massacre_(Australia)#Community_and_government_reaction accessed 2/21/18

47. Leigh A. Why the NRA has Australia in its sights. Sydney Morning Herald, July 14, 2015. http://www.smh.com.au/comment/why-the-nra-has-australia-in-its-sights-20150714-gic1a6.html accessed 2/21/18

48. Dudley et al, *op. cit.*
49. Chapman S, Alpers P, Jones M. Association between gun law reforms and intentional firearm deaths in Australia, 1979-2013. JAMA 2016;316(3):291-299
50. Gun laws in Australia. Wikipedia https://en.wikipedia.org/wiki/Gun_laws_in_Australia accessed 2/21/18
51. Heard on NPR in the days after Parkland, but backed by: Smith A. Obama is the best gun salesman in America. CNN Money January 6, 2016 http://money.cnn.com/2016/01/06/news/obama-gun-control-sales/index.html accessed 2/23/18
52. Potok M. The year in hate and extremism. SPLC, February 17, 2016 https://www.splcenter.org/fighting-hate/intelligence-report/2016/year-hate-and-extremism accessed 7/10/16
53. Hofstadter R. America as a gun culture. American Heritage 1970 21(6) http://www.americanheritage.com/content/america-gun-culture accessed 2/19/18
54. For polls and more details, see: Kristof N., *op. cit.*
55. Fox L. NRA's Wayne LaPierre hits Democrats, socialism in speech that goes beyond gun fight. CNN, February 22, 2018, https://www.cnn.com/2018/02/22/politics/wayne-lapierre-cpac-speech-nra/index.html accessed 2/22/18 and ABC World News Tonight 2/22/18
56. Stroebe *et al*, *op. cit.*
57. Loughran TA, Reid JA, Collins ME, Mulvey EP. Effect of gun carrying on perceptions of risk among adolescent offenders. Am J Pub Health. 2016 106(2):350-352

58. Feldmann, TB, Johnson PW. The selfobject function of weapons: a self psychology examination. J Am Acad Psych 1992 204(4):561-576
59. Lapierre MA, Farrar KM. Learning to love guns? Gun-based gameplay's links to gun attitudes. Psych Pop Media Cult. 2016 1-15
60. Zhang, S. Why can't the U.S. treat gun violence as a public health problem? The Atlantic. February 15, 2018 https://www.theatlantic.com/health/archive/2018/02/gun-violence-public-health/553430/ accessed 2/26/18
61. Diener E, Kerber KW. Personality characteristics of American gun-owners. 1979 J Soc Psych 107:227-238
62. Cunningham PB, Henggeler SW, Limber SP, Melton GB, Nation MA. Patterns and correlates of gun ownership among nonmetropolitan and rural middle school students. J Clin Child Psych 2000, 29(3):432-442
63. Shapiro JP, Dorman RL, Burkes WM, Welker CJ, Clough JB. Development and factor analysis of a measure of youth attitudes towards guns and violence. J Clin Child Psych. 1997, 26(3):311-320
64. Erle TM, Barth N, Kälke F, *et al*. Are target-shooters more aggressive than the general population? Aggressive Behav. 2017, 43:3-13
65. Berkowitz L, LePage A: Weapons as aggression-eliciting stimuli. J. Personal. Soc. Psychol. 1967, 7:202-207 http://dx.doi.org/10.1037/h0025008
66. Benjamin AJ, Bushman BJ. The weapons effect. Curr Opin Psych 2018,19:93-97
67. Carter *et al*, *op. cit.*

68. Filindra A, Kaplan NJ. Racial resentment and white's gun policy preferences in contemporary America. Political Behav. 2016, 38:255-275
69. O'Brien K, Forrest W, Lynott D, Daly M. Racism, gun ownership and gun control: biased attitudes in US Whites may influence policy decisions. 2013, PLoS ONE 8(10):E77552. doi:10.1371/journal.pone.0077552 accessed 2/25/18
70. Stroebe *et al*, *op. cit.*
71. For polls and more details, see: Kristof N., *op. cit.*
72. Christoffel KK, Naureckas SM. *op. cit.*
73. Healy J. 'It's one of the greatest rifles': fans of the AR-15 explain the gun's appeal. New York Times, February 20, 2018 https://www.nytimes.com/2018/02/20/us/ar-15-owners html accessed 2/20/18
74. Maccar D. The most popular guns on Gun Broker in 2015. Range365, January 13, 2016 https://www.range365.com/most-popular-guns-on-gun-broker-in-2015 accessed 2/20/18
75. Surowiecki J. Taking on the NRA. The New Yorker, October 19, 2015. https://www.newyorker.com/magazine/2015/10/19/taking-on-the-n-r-a accessed 2/20/18
76. Timmons H. The NRA invested millions in these politicians in 2016. Quartz, February 14, 2018. https://qz.com/1207851/parkland-shooting-the-nra-and-gun-lobby-invested-millions-in-trump-and-other-republicans-in-2016/ accessed 2/20/18
77. Jacobson L. Counting up how much the NRA spends on campaigns and lobbying. Politifact, October 11, 2017 http://www.politifact.com/truth-o-meter/

article/2017/oct/11/counting-up-how-much-nra-spends/ accessed 2/20/18
78. Parker K *et al, op. cit.*
79. Associated Press. The latest: Trump criticizes active-shooter drills in school. Washington Post, February 22, 2018 https://www.washingtonpost.com/politics/federal_government/the-latest-ny-lawmaker-links-mass-murderers-democrats/2018/02/21/f59bacec-176f-11e8-930c-45838ad0d77a_story.html accessed 2/21/18
80. Tenhundfeld NL, Parnes JE, Conner BT, Witt JW. Develoopment of a psychometrically valid gun attitude scale. Current Psych. 2017

Acknowledgments

THANKS TO THE MANY researchers and journalists whose work informed this essay. Without your efforts, I would not have been able to write these words. I hope the general public and policymakers also pay close attention to your knowledge and observations. Thanks also to my friends and colleagues who offered their thoughts in conversations on this important subject.

About the Author

RAVI CHANDRA, M.D. is a psychiatrist and author in San Francisco. He is a Distinguished Fellow of the American Psychiatric Association, and a graduate of Brown University and Stanford University School of Medicine. He did his residency training in Psychiatry at the University of California, San Francisco, which included work at the Veterans Administration Medical Center in San Francisco and the San Francisco General Hospital in addition to the UCSF hospital. He has written the *Pacific Heart* blog for *Psychology Today* since 2011, and the *Memoirs of a Superfan* film blog for the Center for Asian American Media since 2006. In March, 2016, he was the beneficiary of a Proclamation by the Board of Supervisors of San Francisco, honoring him for his activities in the Asian American community.

This essay is adapted from the forthcoming book *American Identity Crisis: Narcissism, Tribal-*

ism, the Power Complex, Insecurity and Transcendence in the Trump (and Post-Trump) Era, to be published in September, 2018. Sign up for an occasional newsletter at his writer website for details on this and other future writing projects and events.

Writer website: www.RaviChandraMD.com
Private practice website: www.sfpsychiatry.com
Facebuddha: www.facebuddha.co
Compassion and self-compassion workshops:
www.SFLoveDojo.org
Twitter: @going2peace
Instagram: @ravichandramd
Facebook: www.facebook.com/SanghaFrancisco/

Other Books by Ravi Chandra

Facebuddha:
Transcendence in the Age of Social Networks

Asian American Anger: It's A Thing!

a fox peeks out: poems

American Identity Crisis:
Narcissism, Tribalism, the Power Complex,
Insecurity and Transcendence
in the Trump (and Post-Trump) Era
(Forthcoming, 2018)

Indivisible:
A South Asian American Poetry Anthology
(contributor)

www.ingramcontent.com/pod-product-compliance
Lightning Source LLC
Chambersburg PA
CBHW020301030426
42336CB00010B/858